Sweaty Cats
and
Baby Pigeons

Alan L. Simons
Illustrated by Ellen van Boggelen-Heutink

Baronel Books
Toronto, Canada

Sweaty Cats and Baby Pigeons

This edition 2013
Text Copyright © 2013 Alan L. Simons.
Illustrations Copyright © 2013 Ellen van Boggelen-Heutink.

Sweaty Cats and Baby Pigeons has its own website: http://sweatycats.info

Library and Archives Canada Cataloguing in Publication

ISBN 978-0-987-75036-5

***

Baronel Books
Toronto, Canada

publisher@baronel.info
http://baronel.info

This book is dedicated to

all grandparents, my children and grandchildren

and to my brother

Stephen

Alan L. Simons gratefully acknowledges Rhona Bennett for her invaluable contribution in editing and proofreading the manuscript.

.

The Incredible Adventures of Captain Cameron MacDuddyfunk in Cuggermuggerland, another fine children's book by Baronel Books, can be ordered through retail and online bookstores.
ISBN 978-0-987-75038-9
For details contact: publisher@baronel.info

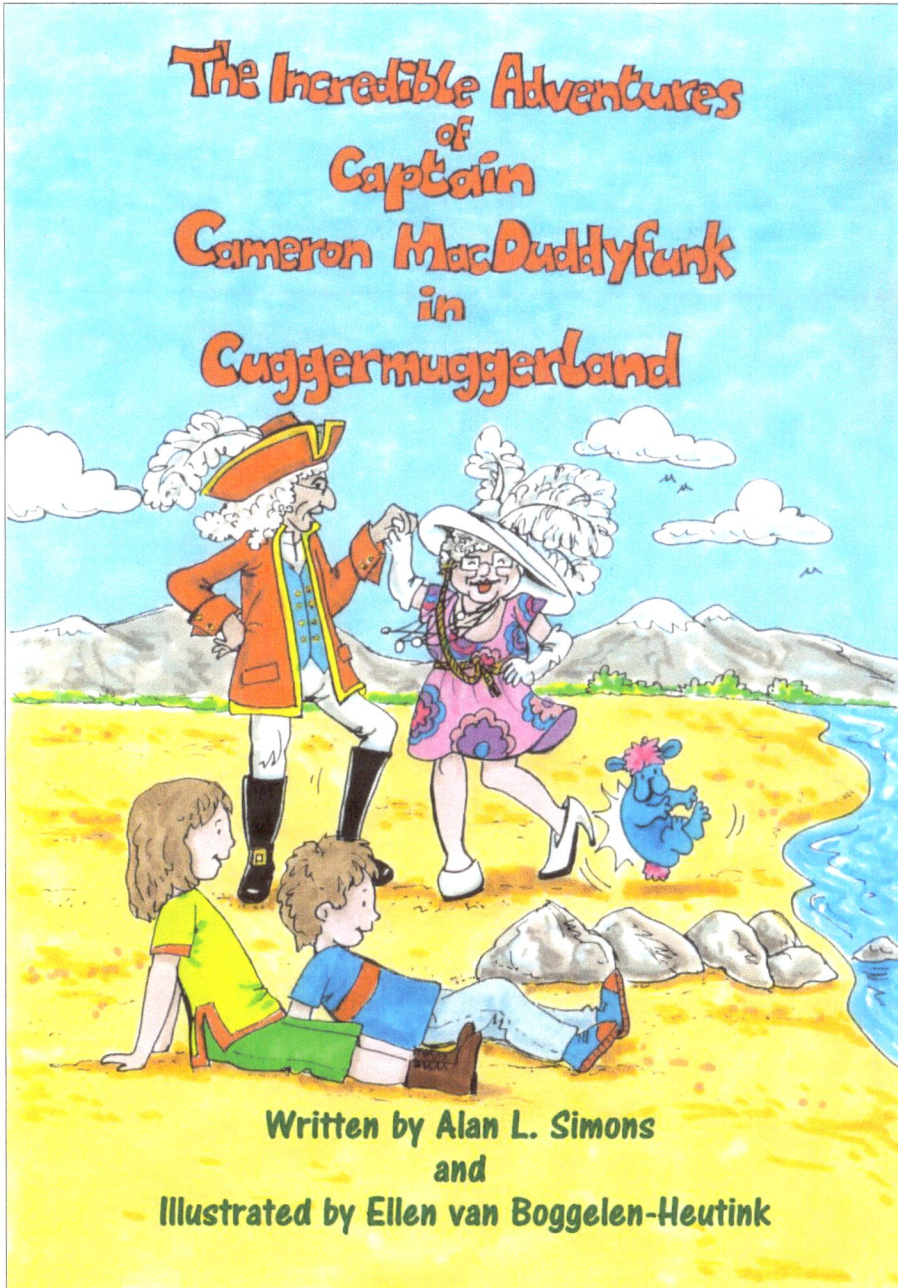

The Incredible Adventures of Captain Cameron MacDuddyfunk in Cuggermuggerland

Written by Alan L. Simons
and
Illustrated by Ellen van Boggelen-Heutink

About the Author

Alan L. Simons was born, raised and educated in London, England, and worked for various newspapers in England. Emigrating to Canada during the Trudeau era, he resumed his career in the newspaper and magazine field and established an advertising and communications company. On the diplomatic scene, he served as Honorary Consul of the Republic of Rwanda to Canada from 1999-2002. He has lectured at numerous institutions in the areas of therapeutic management, communications, religion and politics. After living in Amsterdam for several years, he has now returned to Toronto where is working on his third book, a novel, set in France, which addresses cultural diversity issues that go beyond stereotypes in society. He has appeared on TV, radio and in the print media.

For more information: http://alansimons.info

About the Illustrator

Ellen van Boggelen-Heutink was born in the Netherlands and emigrated with her family to Barrie, Ontario, Canada when she was eight years old. In 1971 she decided to go back to art school in the Netherlands where she met her husband, a ceramist. After their first child was born, they decided that caring for foster children could be combined very well with their work as artists. Ellen did commissions for Sesame Street, Tom and Jerry, Bugs Bunny, etc. and many other companies sprinkled all over the Netherlands. She currently lives with her husband and seven foster children on a farm in Germany and has a studio across the border in the Netherlands. Among many other things, she has written and illustrated a number of children's books for the international market.

For more information: www.ellenheutink.nl

Introduction

These eight short stories are written for the inquiring mind of a young child, with the view that grandparents play an important role in the development of their loved ones.

Many grandparents have had to accept that their grandchildren do not live around the corner from them. Therefore, intensive periods of involvement with them are relatively short. Yet, we still strive at every opportunity, to keep in touch with our grandchildren.

The stories and illustrations that follow are a fun, humourous and expressive way in which grandparents can interact and stimulate communication between the generations, as well as develop a whole series of creative questions. These questions can initiate the first step of an educational journey of discovery.

Alan L. Simons
Toronto, Canada
September, 2013.

SWEATY CATS

How do cats sweat?

When I go out, there are many things I think about, especially when it's a hot day and I get sweaty. I think about sweat.

Sometimes I think about my sweat, underneath my armpits. Sometimes I raise my arms up over my shoulders, put my nose to my armpits, and smell my sweat. It smells very stinky.

It's different from the smell of my stinky socks, or my mouth when I don't brush my teeth.

It's very different from the smell of my mum's

perfume. It's different from the smell of my dog, after he's been playing in some dirty water.

My best friend, Declan, told me that dogs sweat. He told me that when dogs are too hot they start panting with their tongues hanging out. He said that's why you see them running with their tongues hanging out of their mouths on a hot day.

I ask my friend a lot of questions. He doesn't know all the answers, but he's older than I am, and always treats me like a baby. One day, I asked him some questions he didn't know the answers to. I asked him if he knew how a cat sweats. He said he didn't know. I also asked him if he knew how a pigeon sweats. He said he didn't care. I then asked him if he knew how an ant sweats. He got really mad at me and told me that I was stupid. I asked him if he knew how a dinosaur sweated. My friend said that he had had enough of me and was going home. So I went home too.

When I got home, I asked my mum if she knew

how a cat sweats. She told me to go and wash my hands. Why is it that my mum tells me to go and wash my hands when she doesn't answer my questions? Sometimes when I ask her a question she gives me a funny look and just smiles.

Sometimes when I ask my teacher a question she doesn't tell me to go and wash my hands. She smiles at me and tells me to sit down. When that happens, some kids in the class turn around and make funny faces at me. I don't like that. I feel stupid.

When I'm in the school library and ask the librarian a question, she also smiles at me and tells me to go and find the answer by looking it up on the computer. Sometimes, she points to a row of books and tells me I'll find the answer over there. But I don't know where there is!

Why do so many adults just smile when I ask them a question?

Sweat. All I want to know is how a cat sweats.

I have a dog and a cat. My friend told me how my dog sweats, how come he won't tell me how my cat sweats?

Last night, during dinner, my dad said to my mum that the cheese looked as if it was sweating. I asked him how come he knew the cheese was

sweating, but didn't know how a cat sweats. He really got upset with me, and told my mum that she had better do something about her son.

Why is it that when my dad gets upset with me he always tells my mum that I am her son? I thought I was his son too! When my mum is upset with me, she never tells my dad that he had better do something about his son.

I really wish I knew how a cat sweats. I would do anything to find out the answer. I bet my grandparents would know how cats sweat. ☼

BABY PIGEONS

Why have I never seen a baby pigeon?

Every time I go out shopping with my mum and dad I see pigeons. They all look the same to me, dirty. I wonder where they come from. You see them all around the city, on buildings, on roofs and under bridges. I even see them on the pavement pecking at nothing! But I have never seen a pigeon in a tree like all the other birds. I have never heard them sing as other birds do either. And I have never seen a baby pigeon.

I have asked all my friends if they had ever seen a baby pigeon and all my friends said no. My friend Declan, who always knows all the answers, told me that he has never seen a baby pigeon, but his dad told him pigeons are really called rock doves.

I thought that was very funny. I told him that I didn't believe him and that his dad was teasing him. Declan said that his dad never teases him. I said that was very sad because my dad is always teasing me and it's a lot of fun! Sometimes though, I'm not sure when my dad is teasing me and when he's being serious.

I asked my friend what would happen if I asked our teacher if she had ever seen a baby rock dove. I bet she wouldn't know that I was really talking about baby pigeons. My friend said our teacher always smiles and replies by saying, "that's a good question," and "what do you think the answer is."

When I get older, I'll tell my teacher that if I knew the answer, I wouldn't be asking her the question.

My friend said my teacher might speak to my parents about me.

All I want to know is why I've never seen a baby pigeon. I've seen baby ducks swimming in the ponds and in the parks. But I've never seen a baby pigeon.

I want to ask my mum if she has ever seen a baby pigeon, but I think she might tell me to ask my dad. And then he would tease me and say that it's just like my mother's son to ask him that question. He's probably saying that because he's never seen a baby pigeon either!

Why haven't I ever seen a baby pigeon?☼

NAMES

Why can't I choose my own name?

I don't like my name! *Abacuck!* When I get older, I'm going to change my name. It's not fair! My mum and dad picked my name without asking me if I liked it! I wish I could change my name now.

I've told my mum and dad that my friends in school always tease me about my name. My teachers can't spell it either, and the school principal doesn't know how to pronounce it.

I'm really fed up!

My mum tells me that I'm named after her great uncle. I don't think I know what a great uncle is. If my mum's great uncle liked his name so much, he should have kept it. I don't want it! Why did I get it?

My sister, who's only three years old, can't pronounce my name properly. Now everyone pronounces my name the same way she does. "Acuck! Acuck!" I'm really mad!

Why can't kids choose their own name? All my friends have real names like Imogen and Asher and Milo and Harper. One of my new baby cousins was given the name Noah. I like that. Why wasn't I called Noah? No, I had to be named after great uncle Abacuck. He couldn't have been that great!

I want to change my name now. My friends think that is a good idea. I have told my mum and dad, and they said that if I want to do that, I should go ahead and do it.

But I'm not stupid. I know they are fed up with

me whining about my name, and that I should be quiet!

I also hate it when my little sister calls my name out. "Acuck!" Everyone laughs and they all think she is so cute. So she keeps on repeating "Acuck!" to get attention.

On Monday, when I go back to school, I'm going to tell all my teachers that I have changed my name to Noah, and that my parents said that I can do it if I want to. And I am going to tell my teachers that I do not need a note from my parents to change my name.

No! I am not going to wait until I am older to change my name. I am going to do it now! ☼

ANTS

Why can't I have a pet ant?

For as long as I can remember, I've always wanted a pet ant. When I was very young, my mum used to take me to the park and put me on a big blanket with lots of toys.

Sometimes a few ants would come onto the blanket and start touching my toys. They were very curious about my toys. I suppose they wanted to play with them too!

I would try to touch one of the ants with my big finger. But the ants would run away before I could touch them. They were very clever.

Every so often, they would come back and then they would run away again as soon as I tried to catch them. I thought they were very funny.

Ants are just as funny and clever as dogs. Why can't I have a pet ant?

Once, I asked my dad if I could have a pet ant. I didn't quite understand what he said, but I don't think he was too happy. He went running into the other room to my mum and started to tell her that I was at it again. I want to know why I can't have a pet ant.

My friend Declan and his older brother told me once how I could keep an ant from running away. He told me to cut up some fresh ginger, and when I see an ant, I should make a ring around it with the ginger.

My mum was very curious about why I wanted her to cut up some ginger for me. I told her it was because I wanted a pet ant. My mum just said that if it would keep me busy and out of her way, she would cut up as much ginger as I wanted.

A little while later, I saw an ant walking on our kitchen table. So I took the pieces of ginger and made a circle around the ant. It was amazing! The ant began to run from one side of the circle to the other.

I thought the ant was very funny! So, I called my mum to show her what my new pet ant could do. I don't think she was too pleased with me because she started to shout for my dad to come into the kitchen now!

When my dad asked me how I got hold of the ginger, I told him that my mum said that if I would keep out of her way, she would cut up as much ginger as I wanted.

My dad wasn't upset with me, but told my mum it was all her fault, and that she shouldn't have given me the ginger in the first place. Then they started to argue, so I left and went outside to find my friends.

I don't understand my parents. All I want to know is why can't I have a pet ant?☼

MY TEACHER

Why won't my teacher ask me a question?

Why is it that when I put up my hand to answer a question that I know the answer to, my teacher never looks at me? I've tried everything to get my teacher's attention, but she always seems not to notice me. I'm really upset about this.

The other day she asked me a question when I didn't know the answer. Why does she always choose me when I don't know the answer? It's not fair!

I told my mum about it, but she just smiled at me and gave me a big hug. That's not an answer!

Why won't my mum tell me?

It's not as if I'm asking my mum and dad for a cell phone or an iPad, which lots of my friends have. All I want is for my teacher to ask me a question when I know the answer.

I've really tried everything. The other day in class, I stood on my chair and raised my right hand up as high as I could. But my teacher told me I should sit down immediately because I was making a spectacle of myself. I didn't understand her. I don't know what a spectacle is. All the other kids laughed at me. I felt very stupid. So I sat down and didn't raise my hand again for a whole week.

A few days later, my teacher called my mum and said that I was refusing to participate in class. I don't understand what is happening.

I told my friend, Declan, about my teacher calling my mum, and he said that's what teachers do after school ends. Declan said that's because after school ends, teachers get bored and fed up with themselves because they don't have anyone to boss around. So they phone parents to make trouble for the kids they teach. It's not fair!

My dad gets very upset with me when my

teacher calls my mum. Why does my teacher always calls my mum, never my dad? I don't understand why my teacher never wants me to answer a question when I know the answer.

My teacher always lets her favourite kids answer the easy questions. And then she smiles at them, and lets all of us know what wonderful answers they gave. It sucks!☼

MY GRANDPARENTS

Why are my grandparents so old?

I can't figure it out. When I ask my mum and dad how old my grandparents are, they just look at each other and sigh. My mum says that they are old, but I mustn't ask my grandparents how old they are because they'll get upset.

But I wasn't going to ask my grandparents how old they are. I asked my mum and dad. It's always like that. My mum and dad never answer my questions properly.

When I grow up, I'm not going to be like them. If

someone asks me how old my mum and dad are, I'll tell them. I think I will, if I can figure out how old they are. What's the use? I know they won't tell me how old they are.

Why are my grandparents so old? I love them very much. They're always happy to see me and my little sister, and I like the presents they give me.

Sometimes I wish I could go and live with them. They don't tell me not to do things, and my grandmother always cooks the things I like most.

I wish I could change things around, so that my grandparents were my real parents and my real parents became my grandparents. Yes, in that way, maybe my grandparents wouldn't be that old.

I love my grandparents, and my grandfather answers all my questions, but they both smell old, especially my grandfather. I wonder if all grandfathers smell like my grandfather. I asked my friend Declan if his grandfather stinks and my friend said that he didn't know. His grandfather is dead.

So I asked him if his grandmother smells and he said that he couldn't remember because she lives far away in another city, and he hasn't seen her for a very long time. I said that was very sad.

I asked him if he ever speaks to her on Skype or on the telephone, and he said that he didn't want to talk about it anymore.

My grandparents don't live too far away. I don't think they go out too much 'cause whatever time we get to their house, they're always waiting outside for us, and the food is always on the table. So I suppose my grandmother never goes out 'cause she's too busy cooking for us.

It's always the same. Just before we arrive at my grandparents' house my dad tells me not to touch anything and my mum tells me not to forget to give them a big kiss and to take my shoes off before I walk on their white carpet. I'm fed up hearing about their white carpet. It's not white at all. It's creamy looking, and it's old, like all the other stuff in their house.

No, I can't walk with my shoes on my

grandparents' creamy looking carpet, but my baby sister can. No one tells her to take off her shoes. In fact, no one tells her to stop doing anything. It's always me. It's not fair!

I love my grandparents. I wish I could go and live with them. If I did, then I wouldn't need to see my parents sucking up to my baby sister all the time and hear then making stupid baby noises at her.

I'm really, really bored.

How old are my grandparents? If I went to live with them, I bet they would tell me how old they are. And I bet they would know all the answers to my questions.☼

SMOKING

Why do some kids want to smoke?

I hate cigarettes and so do my mum and dad. Sometimes when my dad comes home late at night after attending a meeting, the first thing he does is rush into the bathroom, take his clothes off and have a shower.

He told me that he does that because he's been with some people who have been smoking, and now his hair and all his clothes stink of cigarette smoke. He says that many people he knows smoke cigarettes and they stink too!

My dad says smoking cigarettes is very bad for one's health and that lots of people who smoke get very sick.

I asked my dad why people smoke cigarettes if they know they will get sick. He said that's because many people who smoke have an addiction to it and have difficulty stopping. Then they have to go to the doctor for help and treatment.

My dad said that some people don't believe they will get sick from smoking and continue smoking. He said they are crazy.

One morning while I was eating my breakfast, I asked my mum what an addiction was. She gave me a very strange look and asked me where I had heard that word. I told her my dad had said it when he was talking to me about smoking.

My mum went very quiet and didn't say anything for a while. Then she said an addiction is like wanting things all the time such as eating too many candies.

Then she asked me if anyone had given me a cigarette to try. I said no, but I had seen some of the older boys and girls from my school smoke cigarettes on their way home from school.

I asked my mum if those kids are going to get sick, as my dad had told me. She said yes, there was a good possibility they would get sick if they continued to smoke. And by the time they grow up and be parents, they could become very, very sick.

I asked her why then do they want to keep on smoking. My mum said that they smoke because they think it's cool and want to impress their friends. She said that sometimes, when we are young, we don't want to believe that smoking affects our health, but it does.

I told my mum that I'm never, never, never going to smoke because I hate the stinky smell that people have from smoking, and I don't want to stink like they do, and I don't want to get sick. ☼

WHEN I GROW UP

What am I going to be when I grow up?

I don't know. I'm only a kid. My parents like to ask me what I'm going to be when I grow up.

How do I know what I'm going to be when I grow up?

My best friend, Declan, says that when he grows up, he's going to leave home and work in another city. I asked him what he's going to do there. All he does is shrug his shoulders and say he doesn't care.

But Declan is older than me.

What am I going to do when I grow up? Perhaps

I'll go and live with my grandparents.

How do I know what I'm going to be when I grow up?

My mum says that I will go and work in my dad's office and learn the business. I don't know what the business is, and when I ask my dad what the business is, my mum and dad start laughing at me, and then they start hugging and kissing each other. They always do stupid things like that.

My parents really treat me like a little baby. It's not fair and I'm not stupid. And my baby sister doesn't look like me either.

One of the kids at school says when he grows up he's going to be a doctor like his dad. I hope he doesn't, because his dad is my doctor, and I wouldn't want that kid to shove those sticks in my mouth when I've got a sore throat.

The other day my friend's dad told me that I'm just like my dad, always asking good questions. He said that someday I would take over the business. I also told him that I don't know what the business is, and then he started to laugh at me, just like my parents did.

I'm really getting fed up.

What am I going to be when I grow up? I don't know, and I don't care and I'm not going to care for a long time.

Mum, I'm starving. Can I please have something to eat?☼

www.ingramcontent.com/pod-product-compliance
Lightning Source LLC
Chambersburg PA
CBHW060832270326
41933CB00002B/60